A Little Song

First Published in 2025

ISBN 978-93-342-4010-8

Cover design and illustrations by: Ritika Verma

A Little Song

"The world breaks everyone, and afterward, some are strong at the broken place."

- Ernest Hemingway

Contents

Introduction

If you think the poems in this book are merely imagination, you will find that partially false. The deep, dark stories first happened, then were imagined. Each hero in this book wants to sing their grim fairy tale. They cannot be alone in the time and place they are. Nobody can judge why they did what they had to.

Let me first tell you about the man who got up to go on an adventure but forgot to take the wheels off his chair. He may not be able to go at all because unexpectedly it started to rain, even though he had packed his matchstick, cigar, and pain. Meanwhile, elsewhere, Oliver Fain was drowning in the ocean, although he had been thinking and planning rightly from the start about how to save the tanner. But while saving him, he didn't plan to save himself from the ocean.

The words within may twist your mind and linger long after you've turned the page. Proceed with caution, for once you enter, there may be no way back.

If you would not be there

I surely not be here

my name sits on this page

as your praise

my imagination comes to life

as you pick your pencil and drive

Special thanks to my sister

Ritika Verma who did the art.

Preface

The very first lines I comprehend

But only the first lines

The poem I find difficult

Is not very fine

The images and knoll

I found them all

I thought there were three

Besides you and we

In this world of wonder

Too obvious the tittle for thunder

I might a layman

To find the rhyme

The poems I find difficult

Is not very fine

                              Payal Verma

Bella Crown

There was this little boy whose

Name was Bella Crown

I once was a girl, and my mother always

frown

Bella crown was a boy and

hanging on a branch

Outride travelling stranger,

With an open Franch

'how could you get so high

- just above the tranche?'

the boy replied, 'mother is a finch

Well played the game!

now I must be ditched

each man I get to tranche

well, you see

just below the branch

This is your turn

stranger,

come and help me down

we take turn who gets the crown

the boy must be at home the mother sees

through slit

the boy with the stranger coming with a

grit

the three ate together

on the dinner table

man's crown sits

on the abandoned fable

Up The River

Up the river until the swamp

There comes the little boy

Who goes for the farm

Biscuits, bread and butter, and jam

Collecting into his little arm

Up the river, until the Cliff

There goes a straight road

With a side sudden flip

Followed through the right and left

Confused little boy, it's damp and dark,

Road goes to the west and eastern farm

Farm is where sweet and warmth

Up the river until the lamp

Flickering light about to be stamped

Found the road with mother's arms

He'll be home in no time at all

up the river in a small cottage inside

boy makes the toast

blue and cold her mother lies

Unmatched Socket

Right over in his hands

He saw drunken suddenness

Shivering in the right hand old

He couldn't stop his lost soul

Lantern lit with a dim light

Hour struck the dead night

Right over in his coat pocket

He found an unmatched socket

Fill the pot and heat the kettle

He remembered with a sudden rattle

Where's the maiden to bring him tea

Must go home in windy spree

First moon light the socket

Red and feisty, numb and nasty

Must go home in such hasty

Tea must have gone cold

kettle was so old

knocked at the door

maiden was no more

he thought to bore

right at the door she sleeps

where's the maiden to bring him tea

Oliver Fain

Oliver fain was right in the brain

Went to the sea and shore

There he saw a little girl diving

Who once was up and bore

Oliver fain was right in the brain

Went straight and dived in a manner

But only he knew how to swim

Just like the girl with the tanner

Oliver fain was right in the brain

water was up his crown

the little girl was near and far

and fain knew not to drown

One Ounce Bread

Standing in the street

He thought to himself

Should he buy butter or one-ounce

bread,

Looking down the slope

Bread was too much to buy

his empty stomach squibbed

had a dime to try,

Butter was farthest and bread was close

Though he had nothing to lose,

Bread was desired and butter was toast

That is what his mother said,

He took his dime and reached the shop

Emptied his pocket to the top,

there he stood with his heart in hands

for the dime was too less for

one-ounce bread,

so, he bought the butter one spoonful

happy little child who's no fool

A Girl and The Bale

A fairy tale, a girl and the bale

Waited long in the land of stale

No prince passed those lines

Not ever crossed the climbs

She waited too long, too long of an age

Bale on her head in the land of stale

She waited too long till sixteen

No prince came during the gleams

Silver haired fox, she shone brightly

But no prince came that she blames

She waited too long in the land of stale

but still no prince came

at last, she put the bale

on her husband's dale

sighed but no prince came

Granny's Home

Granny's home is not to be find

For she has always keep it behind

It is about corner and near

we will all be lost I fear,

she's living there for past 50 years

I stumble whenever I hear

Talks about the home all the time

How she moved it and named it Ryne,

Hard to forget, it looked so sleek

Vibrant colors and freedom to be meek

Must find it soon we are in despair

Tired and wired, it's so hard to bear,

Granny's still talking close to my ear

That she lived in a beautiful home

And it must have been near

Round and round we walked every

corner

Her dream never seems to begin shorter

Philby At Heaven's Gate

Philby was stopped at heaven's gate

Questioned Philby, "why ain't I

allowed?"

Replied the keeper, "do good deeds

eleven-

to enter, you are undeservedly proud",

In confusion, Philby asked

"what's with eleven, not ten or seven,"

He did some great ones if not many

Donated tons and never wronged any,

Soon a man entered with a number ten

Doubted Philby, if he bribed the

middleman,

"Let me go in, aghast

Lot of money I earned at last",

Though his pockets were at length

Still difficult to fill them after death,

Insisted Philby, "how the man was

allowed?"

Keeper said, "do good deeds eleven

you're undeservedly proud"

Fragrance Of Smoke

Life comes, life goes,

What stays is

Fragrance of my father's smoke,

Sweet, musky still hard and husky

Pale, silver like a smoking husky

Figuring solemnly deep of the bloke

Fragrance of my father's smoke,

knocked at the door never even rang the

bell

journeying into already blurred eyes

got his feet swelled,

Oh! That exhilarated smell

Smoke makes passes on all the lies,

Easy life, happy life at fifty-two

Crutches become fragile with all the

stew,

Fragrance of my father's smoke

Soon took place of only left soul

Still diving deep of the bloke

Treacle

There once was a man lived in a

cupboard

Filled with all the treacle,

No one ever saw him out

So, the man not to be at drought

Love made him live in closet

The world outside was without faucet

Only if something could quench his thirst

He would have seen the world

The fear of leaking faucet at high

Always slammed the door to say nigh

Many tried to take him out

The man was not to be sought

Some says he still lives there

Some claims gone somewhere

Oldest man who is oldest of all

Swears cupboard still have treacle of all

Different

Different lived in indifferent world

Where nobody could answer his swirl

Confused about his uncanny difference

But nothing he gained from inference,

Last an old lady thought for a while

Whether she could tell him a lie

A story of indifferent who never

Cared for living in a different world

Never asked and never feared

Listening to this he thought,

"If I am doing it wrong"

World was indifferent so not to be

different

All are same and happy and twirl

Without making each other whirl

Different still lives in indifferent world

With no questions about his swirl

Mrs. Wilson, Too Loud

Too loud, too loud

Mrs. Wilson was too loud

In her room she stays

Quiet and calmed

Outside she's too loud

Goes in and out, whether free or stout

Rather she was too loud

If you ask her name

if you are fast or lame

cry or weep, pray or sleep

Mrs. Wilson always too loud

The quieter around the louder she

sounds

Confused being shrill or aloud

She snores too loud

Even she pores too loud

At times Mrs. Wilson yells

There is noise in her head

Snaggy hearing her own gnarly voice

She is just too loud

Madame Limiti

Madame Limiti lived her life

In search of heaven and light

Did she find it?

She claims, yes

It's in her multiple objects

In the shoes and the hymns

In the flattery and the grins

God is in you and me

So, she frowns whenever it please

Madame Limiti's heaven is there

In the room where she glares

Maids, housekeepers and the priest

Know her to be polite and free

Free from all anticipation and worries

She knows no limit

Could fly in the finite

She knows all the best for you and me

Its's her and her god

She can debate any minute

The Case of Muttering Mouse

The Muttering Mouse

goes to mutter

in a very low voice

to irritate others

all his friends

spoke high

but the muttering mouse

couldn't comply

The Muttering Mouse

goes to mutter

and tell a secret

he knows

all his friends

who spoke high

were not about

to blow

The Muttering Mouse's

friends are loyal

this is true for sure

all his friends

like cats disguised

the secret was

to devour

The Muttering Mouse

pledges not to mutter

to fake friends anymore

but all his friends

were on the way

to stop the

squeak evermore

Pumpy Poo

Pumpy poo lived under the sea

Under great pressure of gigantic sea

Fat and flaky, sounds like glee

Sovereign bond with all in need

Pumpy poo lived under a rock

The rock under a ship dock

The pressure and noise of daily hassle

He thought of strewing it to his debtors

Pumpy poo lived in a shoe

Someone recalled it was blue

In the great blue shoe, he was unseen

He ordered a Pictor to turn it green

Pumpy poo had ten hands together

But all tied in a polished manner

In riches and jewel slaying on the soul

Pumpy the squid blemished the shoal

After galloping a thousand and seventy-

three fishes

Weeny Pumpy wagging through his

riches

Pumpy wanted the lion's mane

fish did turn him into a golden flame

Blind Birds

Listen to the birds, blind in the eyes

Fate has upon them moved in a twill

No see, no hear, not even minute fear

Singing through the ocean and

through the wood

Singing in the upland at the top of the

roof

Wearily they stirred in the shadow of

their own

Singing through the night and the dusty

storm

The light and the shrill, make no twitch

Only their melody with the perfect glitch

The fire and shire,

they moved through the mire

The blind birds were no dumb or numb

They felt the heat

Over the ocean in a sudden steam

Forgotten Wheels

In his chair, he sits upon

He thinks, of the moment, he wears it on

A clock of tranquil, he was ready to fight

Thinking of his various flights

Might go to the river, to the forest, to

the dump

He might wear a fussy cap to mask his

clump

As soon as he gets up, he forgets to

take

Wheels of the chair to accompany his

trail

He packed his pain, but it started rain

Took all unnecessary slain

His flight is delayed for one more time

Still bagged the things he liked

A dumper, water, and a plant of rotten

A matchstick and a cigar left no

unforgotten

He mounted his chair and his wheels

To take the flight in the rim made of

steel

Fire In the Woods

A fire in the woods

ashes and rain

Burning upon the woods

Like a demon in trame,

The demon wants to go wherever it can

Lost in the search of heaven or hell,

He found the place

The place before the end,

Pain and suffering, tranquility and

deafening

Burning in fire with peace and toil

Fire demon found the hell

and it's just the place to soil

Tither

Tithes I pay for my bread

Comes at the cost of sinfulness,

I pray, I bow, I do make the way

Which goes directly into my grave,

I live in the world of forgetfulness

Where trees play music of unworthiness

I am a tither

Who pays tithe for wither,

The slumping tree and flumping water

Told me a tail of cruel slaughter,

One day a man asked them for

All the food and water at stake,

The humble man got everything they had

he also took their sentience

And I paid my tithe in the end

A Ship Long Docked

A ship to be sailed

Never a ship to be bunkered long

A ship long docked

Never a ship to be sailed along,

Slight storms make it wreck

Smashed against its own deck

Soon comes the time the wreckage sunk

And the qualms of being alone,

Free of all the voyages

Never got hurt in the midst of the storm

What left was not afraid of the dead

Silent came long before sinking head,

Endured tempest but dreaded squall

Homely dock was still to be stalled

A riotous sound makes the end

Ship long docked lies entrenched

Rain Man

I saw a man, raining like a rain man

Wetting all his clothes, and feeling like

no one knows,

Wet and wet, he is always wet,

Wherever he goes, he couldn't rest,

if only the sun shines, he could stop his

whines

But nothing he could do, as there is

always ado,

Long gusty winds, so he couldn't keep

his feet

only if he can retreat, would be a

delicious treat,

Flood's coming only over him

He swamped suddenly into it,

Rain and rain, nothing could stop it

Still wetting his clothes, feeling like no

one knows

There I saw the man

Raining like a rain man

Lioness

In the deep, dark corner

Lioness is sleeping sound,

Though tough bars she was caged in

Wouldn't stop her to growl,

The thought of wilderness

The grass and the pray

Makes her agitated when she's

Mistaken for a stray,

Plan she devised to come out of the bars

Not very long it was seen as hoax,

Brave and gusty, she hauled the fence

Shaking and trying to hold her stance,

Running all mighty she hit the wall

a very strong crude makes up the hall,

a pond to drink and a moat at the brink

there sleeps sound the lioness in her

dream

Walls of Old

Walls of old have seen all those

Hiding what no one was told,

Shrill never got out in plain

Suffering from severe blows,

Hard and stood there never

Moved an inch, up and high

But nearly touching the made-up sky,

All that concrete and bricks alive

As much as still,

Figuring, fazing pounding dime

Olden walls have spied in time,

Daubed in vain to hide pain

Walls of old are plastered

To hide again

The Castle from Childhood

I was hiding in the nest

Which I built out in the west

The western front in my castle

Not with saree but with satchel,

Little one found me

But afraid of the dark

Not in the mood to try hard

Hide and seek it is or hide and found

I remember I played till the dawn,

We two were there sometimes where

Mother would say 'you would go

nowhere'

The kitchen I cooked on the top

Up the cupboard where we loft

Most adventurous of anytime

We slid down in Narnian times

Fancied living in the land

Where only we two

and nothing spans

The Consequence of Being an Introvert

I sat down and asked for a cup of tea

The moment I realized time to flee

I saw men drinking their cup

Still asking and never got heard

All of a sudden somebody came to my

mind

Talking to me for a bounty of time

One or two words

I lost him in third

Hibbity dibbity doo, was all I heard

Dreaming of place not in this time

That miser still asking for something of

mine

Four or five times spying something for

thirst

This was the consequence of being an

introvert

I am an introvert

My brain played a show

No person could tell

The secret better not be blew

A story I thought of, in the meanest of

time

Very next moment I heard him, goodbye

That ended well, ha! What a relief

Oh! Six more persons I forgot to greet

Fireflies

Free fire flies, free as they were

Seem so neat, frequently in a blur

They live in the dangle of

light and black

Darkness has its tale upon the nest

Fire flies as high as it could

Only to be taken into darkness' amath

It molded the fly into his color

The color of no light, certainly

Not the fireflies' bright

Dark Night, No Moon

Starry night, no bloom

Dark night, no moon

I wonder where at you

Darkness makes me search

Vast ocean of pearls

So deep I can't reach you

I still look for you up and above

Ring of fire is not what you

Whither and tither, seems so true

Dark and damp, black and bold

Starry night, but no bloom

Dark night, but no moon

Still, I wonder where at you

Francis

Francis waited for him to come

the longer she waited

the longer he took

the longer she waited

she waited and waited

Nor for her nor for him

but for the love

he spelled on her

In the time

she was fat or small

Sometimes tough or blob

she cried or sighed

Though Francis was tough

but the distance from love

was very rough

Francis waited day or night

looking by her window

on the straight high

The highland between him and Francis

Francis waited long

longer she can imagine

it was her and her

Old house abandoned

She seemed distressed

all the passersby, said

What could be it?

it's the wait for him

who knows him

he's never seen

it's the Francis toil

Who believes in him

Well! I must say

Francis was long awaited

I must not say

she waited in vain or not

but poor Francis

for 13 years has passed

he's still never seen

Francis was never aghast

There was a Girl

There was a girl

who never wore a skirt

She played nothing

Nothing She wrote

Neither she beautiful nor she smart

Neither intelligent

nor even clart

The girl wore pants

in the entire village

her pants were a fuss

who never wore a skirt

There was a girl

who didn't play violin

her singing was not so good

just like her high mood

There was a girl

who never wore a skirt

Nor even her mother

could find it as mirth

The girl cooked nothing

not even stew

Cleaning was not her cake

as it was due

What would she do

her life was ado

her mother panicked all

times, whenever she flew

She found the Dumb

The king asked her to come

with three things to be done

One was none

Other was dumb

She might know the other one

but it was slumb

The order no one could defy or the king

would die

else all loved the beloved king

in the free will or supreme

Let's come back to her

back in her hideous hut

None was easy

What was dumb?

While in the meantime

She was brewing slumb

Big rat's cat

And the jasmine flower

root of pepper

and the soil of tower

None and Slumb were ready

to delay the king's tragedy

What was dumb?

What was dumb?

thinking she began to numb

The king might die

Certainly die

Without dumb he would cry

with three things to be done

She must run

its morning since night

2 pm till the king survives

Else all loved the mighty king

who wanted only three things

She took none and slumb

with her bag and broom

Still thumping her head

about the dumb she couldn't groom

she flew to the king's Chamber

handed him none

the King drank the Slumb

Where was dumb?

The king, the queen,

the priest and the minister

looked funnily at the Sinister

still waiting

for the dumb to come

So, the King can live up to his numb

But the witch couldn't clear

the king was very dear

that no dumb could be made

and the king was about to fade

All five still exists

in the castle of King

If you visit the kingdom

must visit the king

he might find his dumb

and you must not resist

The Prince and the Beast

Long ago he had a plan

to bring his hand into the clan

he travelled east to challenge beast

with valor courage and feet,

up and up above the surge,

a mighty fear with no man touch

soon may he enter lair

to find something with a dark flair

the beast not there to serve the man

he found it insulting and waited till ten

at last the beast came,

The man started upon with rage

beast asked fervently

why you kill me?

he answered

"you are a beast, no friend of man

I will take your head

to my clan

The clan belongs to me

I shall be the king and, wife shall be

queen"

Beast smiled and asked him to sit down,

You must be tired after all this frown

many men came before you

all good men with the mighty hand,

the valor, the courage, the mighty

but were before the almighty

I too traveled east to take on the beast

but no beast came till I waited ten

I am waiting since

like you and other four prince

we all shall wait for the beast to come

Would you like to have some rum

The Last Tale

Each poem tells a tale,

with memories might be pale,

in the state of feeling quiet

all heroes intertwined

the poem rests on the page

too tired to see the face

let it rest it is twenty-eight

each poem tells a tale

tale of old or tale of sake

though you see front and back

I must reveal the

girl with the bale